Detlef Mix

MANUKA HONEY

The all-round talent from New Zealand
for your health and wellbeing

360° medien

LEGAL INFORMATION
Manuka Honey
The all-round talent from New Zealand for your health and wellbeing
Detlef Mix

© 2021 360° medien
Nachtigallenweg 1 I 40822 Mettmann
360grad-medien.de

Haftungsausschluss und allgemeiner Hinweis:
Disclaimer and general information:

The contents presented here are for neutral information and general further education. They do not represent any recommendation or advertisement of the diagnostic methods, treatments or (medicinal) remedies referred to herein. The text is in no way intended to replace the professional advice of a doctor, alternative practitioner or pharmacist, and it may not be used as a basis for independent diagnosis or the commencement, modification or termination of treatment of diseases. If you have any questions, you should always consult your doctor or healthcare provider. The publisher and author assume no liability for any loss or damage resulting from the use of the information presented herein. The publisher and author also assume no liability for the content herein, especially with regard to its accuracy or reliability. The assertion of claims of any kind is hereby excluded.

Editing and proofreading (German): Christine & Andreas Walter

Typesetting and layout: Serpil Sevim-Haase

Illustrations: Carina Engelmann, Maraccuja Grafikdesign, www.maraccuja.de

Translation: Übersetzungsbüro Perfekt GmbH I 81669 München

Printed and bound:
Lensing Druck GmbH & Co. KG I Feldbachacker 16 I 44149 Dortmund
www.lensingdruck.de

Photo credits: 360° medien S. 11; ©LIGHTFIELD STUDIOS - stock.adobe.com S. 31; ©closeupimages – stock.adobe.com S. 35; Beate Dodeck S. 109, 111, 112, 115, 117; iStockphoto.com S. 53, Manuka Health, Umschlag, S. 6/7, 12/13, 15, 26/27, 50/51, 71, 72/73, 75, 76, 78/79, 103 Neuseelandhaus S. 8, 18/19, 74, 104/105, 107

ISBN: 978-3-96855-286-6
Made in Germany

360grad-medien.de

Detlef Mix

MANUKA HONEY

The all-round talent from New Zealand
for your health and wellbeing

360° **medien**

CONTENTS

Manuka honey in action for your health 6

A special plant, an extraordinary honey 12

Manuka honey – for eating and treating 18

Getting the best out of Manuka 21

Don't hold back, honey...25

Taking Manuka - the honey on everyone's lips............26

Mouth...28

Nose and sinuses 30

Inhalation 35

Throat and respiratory tract.......................................37

Oesophagus 39

Stomach... 41

... and gut 44

Internal organs 46

Liver..46

Kidneys, bladder, prostate 48

Applying Manuka – the honey as treatment 50

Our skin 52

Wounds...53

How does Manuka honey work on wounds?............54

Burns..59

Inflammatory skin conditions.....................................61

Oral herpes..64

Eye inflammations...65

Fungal infections...66

Manuka honey for pets...68

Manuka oil..70

Manuka pioneers in Germany **72**

A to Z of uses **78**

Recipes..**104**

Eating healthily with Manuka....................................106

Last but not least **118**

Manuka honey – the real deal 118

Conclusion 123

Index..**124**

MANUKA HONEY
IN ACTION FOR
YOUR HEALTH

MANUKA HONEY IN ACTION
FOR YOUR HEALTH

"An apple a day keeps the doctor away." In other words, healthy food can help you take less pharmaceuticals. Whoever coined this aphorism would undoubtedly be criticised and sued today for making unsubstantiated medical claims.

A similar fate would no doubt have awaited Hippocrates, the founder of modern medicine, who gave us the Hippocratic Oath that still forms the basis of modern healthcare. He said:

"Let food be your medicine and medicine your food."

I fully support this statement. With Manuka honey, you have a side-effect-free medicine that can be kept in the kitchen cupboard.

I've written some detailed books on this subject. So why am I now also producing this practical manual?

Firstly, there is a plethora of articles available on Manuka honey that seem randomly cobbled-together from the Internet and whose accuracy is often questionable. Some of these claim, for example, that the Maori have been using Manuka honey for centuries – despite the fact that honey bees have only existed in New Zealand since the middle of the nineteenth century.

The original settlers of New Zealand certainly used the Manuka plant (especially its leaves, roots, bark and wood), but it was not until the modern era that beekeeping became established there.

Secondly, there is a deluge of conflicting advice, talking Manuka honey up as a miracle cure on the one hand and telling us to use it only for minor cuts and bruises and to be aware of the ubiquitous counterfeit versions on the other hand.

In fact, Manuka honey can be used for treating larger and chronic wounds, as has been documented countless times, not least thanks to its many years of use at the Klinik Havelhöhe in Berlin. No complications have so far been reported there.

My aim with this manual is to provide you with practical instructions and to help you get results. This

Detlef Mix's standard work on Manuka honey (2nd. ed.)

manual deals with the wide range of internal and external uses of Manuka honey and how you can try them out for yourself. Tips on usage and case studies are also included, as are an A-Z of uses, how to test for quality and counterfeit versions, and a selection of recipes.

But first let us turn to Manuka honey's source of nectar, the Manuka bush itself.

A SPECIAL
PLANT,
AN EXTRA-
ORDINARY
HONEY

A SPECIAL PLANT,
AN EXTRAORDINARY HONEY

Manuka was the name given to the New Zealand tea tree by the Maori. The meaning of the word sadly hasn't been preserved, but perhaps it meant "the plant from which everything can be used", as that is precisely what the Maori did.

The explorer James Cook followed their example and named the plant 'tea tree', as its leaves provided a pleasant-tasting substitute for his usual Ceylon tea. Botanists classified the plant as part of the myrtle family and named it leptospermum scoparium (leptospermum being a genus of the myrtle family). Scoparium, which means 'broom-like', describes the characteristic growth habit of Manuka.

The plant can, if left to its own devices, grow into a human-sized bush or a 15 metre tree. Mostly, however, it takes the form of robust scrub that quickly colonises brownfield terrain. Outside of New Zealand, it is today only found in South Australia, mostly in the wild. This pioneer species used to be a farmer's worst nightmare and avoided by beekeepers.

The hostility to this multi-faceted plant only began to change at the start of the 1990s and has subsequently grown into wholesale endorsement. While the tea and essential oil from the plant continue to be appreciated, it is the honey that has experienced an explosion in popularity, ever since research was published by Prof Peter Molan, in which this hitherto ignored honey was shown to have a powerful antimicrobial effect.

Manuka honey is a special blossom honey derived from the nectar of the Manuka plant. As well as the many healthy nutrients that every honey contains in various proportions, Manuka honey also has a special active antimicrobial element, known as the Unique Manuka Factor (UMF).

Identified in 2006 by food chemists at the TU Dresden led by Prof Thomas Henle, the UMF is determined by levels of the sugar by-product methylglyoxal (MGO). However, this is only produced from its precursor dihydroxyacetone (DHA) as the honey ripens in the combs and during the first months of storage. DHA/DHAP (dihydroxyacetone phosphate) occurs naturally in varying concentrations in the nectar, which is introduced into the combs by the bees after they have processed it. Only about one third of the DHA converts to MGO. This is why Manuka honey has varying levels of active ingredients and different MGO labelling.

Since a natural product can't be standardised, producers aim to achieve a relatively consistent MGO quality by mixing different strengths. The strengths are shown with a plus sign to indicate

DID YOU KNOW?

UMF (Unique Manuka Factor) describes the honey's efficacy, whereas MGO (methylglyoxal) relates to the active ingredient. The UMF needs to be compared against a known antibacterial agent. Manuka honey that has the antibacterial effect of a 10% phenol solution is labelled UMF10+. The MGO claim refers to the actual methylglyoxal content in milligrams per kilogram of honey.

that the value shown is often just a minimum. An MGO100+ contains at least 100 milligrams of methylglyoxal per kilogram of honey.

Genuine Manuka honey produced and bottled in New Zealand can be identified via the MGO symbol and the silver fern symbol. Some manufacturers still use the old term UMF instead of the MGO label. See also the chapter headed 'Last but not least' (p. 118).

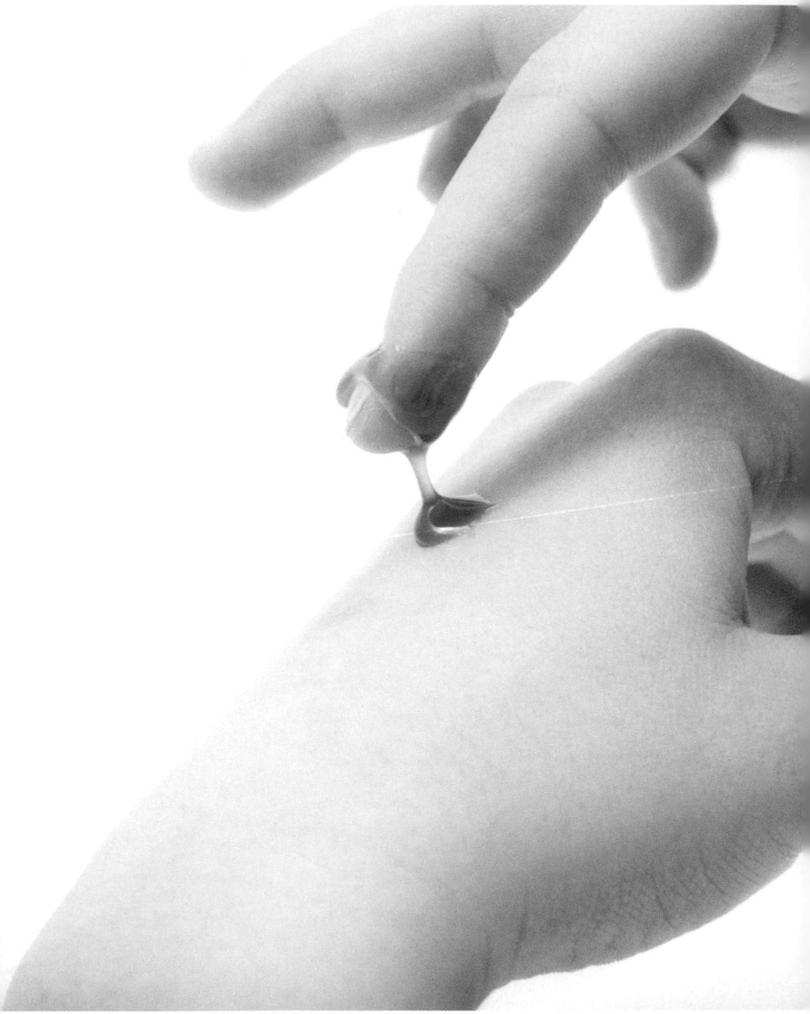

MANUKA HONEY – FOR EATING AND TREATING

MANUKA HONEY – FOR EATING AND TREATING

This is how I describe the versatility of Manuka honey. It is also the title of a lecture that I have given many times to professionals and non-professionals alike.

Before Alexander Fleming discovered penicillin by chance in 1928, honey had long been used in medicine and surgery. Even in the field hospitals of the First World War, not only minor scratches, but also severe wounds and even amputations were treated with a mixture of honey and liver oil. However, with the discovery of antibiotics, this type of usage became less common.

In his Nobel Prize speech in 1945, Fleming warned of the dangers of resistance developing against penicillin. Today, the threat of multi-resistant bacteria is an extremely serious problem worldwide.

In the past three decades, people have been turning once again to honey to fight infection. Manuka honey in particular has often been especially effective in fighting a range of antibiotic-resistant bacteria.

Despite extensive efforts to prove otherwise, Manuka honey has not fallen prey to antibiotic resistance so far. On the contrary, studies in Sydney have suggested that, in bacteria that have become resistant to conventional antibiotics, the honey can actually resensitise the bacteria to the antibiotics.

Some people have asked me whether they could take Manuka honey during a course of antibiotics or chemotherapy. Please be assured that Manuka honey does not interfere with the efficacy of such treatments, but rather enhances them, while significantly reducing unwanted side-effects.

Getting the best out of Manuka Honey
If you want to use Manuka honey as effectively as possible, you don't need to be an expert in anatomy, but an awareness of the body's physiology is always helpful.

For many people, the honey is most of all "intense in price" as Prof Henle stated in an interview. The high cost is mainly due to the complex extraction method used because of the honey's viscosity. Furthermore, Manuka honey cannot be spun like other honey, and it needs to be stirred in a special way to make it creamy and smooth.

Other factors contributing to its price are its short flowering period, the high cost of beekeeping in remote areas and the ever-increasing worldwide demand. Therefore, it is useful to know that you don't necessarily need to choose the most expensive honey, but the most effective MGO value (see MGO value, p. 16).

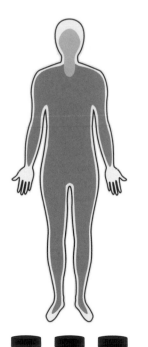

As a rule of thumb, the further you want the honey to penetrate into the body, the more it will become diluted on its journey, and so the stronger it will need to be to start with. Conversely, the shorter the distance to the target area, the less strong (i.e. lower MGO value) the honey needs to be.

For external wounds, you should put the honey directly into the wound or onto a suitable compress and apply a dressing. For such applications, and for any other external use, **MGO100+** is sufficient. In the mouth, nose and throat, **MGO250+** would be required to counteract dilution by saliva and mucous. For deep internal applications (stomach, gut, bladder etc.) you should choose **MGO400+** or stronger.

Some research is based on the honey having an effect beyond mere surface contact with the pathogen or site of inflammation. Nonetheless, your aim should still be to apply the honey directly to the area concerned and to ensure that it stays there for as long as possible.

When the honey comes into contact with the bacteria, its active substances penetrate the bacteria by dissolving their protective 'shells'. As the applicant of the honey, you are therefore having a decisive effect on this process. The honey will certainly have some effect even if you simply ingest it three times a day like any other medicine. This will probably boost your immunity and can be easily incorporated into your diet (for recipe ideas, see p. 104). However, if your aim is to treat a specific acute or chronic prob-lem in the body, then you need to think about how the honey will get to its destination.

For example, how can you ensure that, when you rinse your nose with a Manuka honey solution, you hold your head in the right position so that the solution penetrates the sinuses? How can you use the laws of gravity to coat the stomach, throat or oesophageal membranes with honey? The slow but steady passage of small amounts of honey, perhaps even when you're lying down, would certainly be more effective than simply swallowing a teaspoon of honey two or three times a day. A classic 'Roll-kur' (moving into different positions after ingestion, see gastrointestinal application) with Manuka honey could help to treat gastric inflammation caused by helicobacter pylori, as the harmful bacteria would be prevented from moving into areas where the honey wouldn't otherwise reach.

Don't hold back, honey

The recommendation to take a teaspoon of honey in the morning and evening is usually based on an understandable desire to cut costs. However, I'm not convinced it makes sense to prolong a treatment unnecessarily by dosing the precious substance too carefully. If your house is on fire, saving water will probably be the least of your concerns.

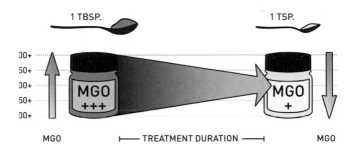

At the beginning of treatment, and especially in the case of severe infections and inflammations, a more generous dose, about a tablespoon, and a higher MGO rating would be advisable. Once symptoms have improved, both can be reduced, but you should continue to take the honey until the condition has cleared up.

TAKING
MANUKA –
THE HONEY ON
EVERYONE'S
LIPS

TAKING MANUKA – THE HONEY ON EVERYONE'S LIPS

Mouth

Manuka honey can distinguish between friend and foe, so its antibiotic effect is selective. It eliminates pathogenic bacteria, while healthy bacteria – the oral and intestinal flora – are not only spared but actually supported. Manuka is therefore well suited to the treatment of infections and inflammations in the mouth, whether bacterial, viral or fungal. You should rinse your mouth before using the honey, but don't brush your teeth directly before or after.

You can apply Manuka honey MGO250+ directly to the infected or inflamed area, for example, to mouth ulcers (Aphthous stomatitis). Use your clean finger to apply the honey. You can also put a teaspoon of the honey in your mouth and keep it there as long as possible.

The osmotic property of honey – the sugar it contains draws water – will lead to saliva building up in your mouth. Keep the resulting honey solution in the area of inflammation. If the entire oral cavity is affected, draw the honey solution through the teeth and rinse your mouth. Eventually, you will reach the point where your mouth is so full that you have to swallow, but you should neither spit out the saliva nor swallow it quickly. Simply let it trickle slowly down your throat.

"The path is the goal." With Manuka, you can often treat ailments that lie en route to the honey's ultimate destination further inside the body.

CASE STUDY

A woman from Austria told me that while she was successfully treating her frequent bladder infections with Manuka, she was at the same time helping her bleeding gums, which had plagued her for many years. She achieved this by not swallowing the honey, but by keeping it in her mouth for as long as possible, as described above.

Since a variety of microbes are sensitive to Manuka, there is also no need to determine the type of pathogen you want to treat, as would be the case before taking antibiotics. Inflammation of the mouth (stomatitis) caused by microbial infections can also be treated with the honey.

This also applies to gingivitis and periodontitis (inflammations of the gums). The honey doesn't care which pathogens are responsible for these conditions. However, you should give it direct contact with them. Apply the honey to the immediate vicinity of the infection and make sure it stays there for as long as possible.

Nose and sinuses

Our breathing should preferably be done through the nose. In contrast to mouth breathing, nasal breathing offers clear benefits. The air is filtered and heated in the nose and we can smell toxic gases before we are harmed by them.

However, this sophisticated ventilation system is often disturbed. Everyone has probably had a

common cold, usually due to a viral infection, where the nasal mucous membranes become irritated and swollen and mucus production increases.

Application using the finger

If you apply Manuka honey directly into your nose, you can usually quickly put an end to this annoying condition, or at least make it more bearable. Draw warm water through your nose and then blow your nose thoroughly. Then put some Manuka honey MGO250+ on your little finger, insert it deeply into both nostrils and pull it up. By pinching your nose, you can distribute the honey even more evenly.

However, if the symptoms persist for weeks or even months and both infection and inflammation spread to the surrounding pockets (sinuses), then you probably have chronic sinusitis (rhinosinusitis).

Now we are no longer dealing with just a viral infection, but with bacteria that like to get into the bed made by viruses. There, they snuggle into a slimy biofilm that antibiotics can't penetrate, and we are sick of it. Hope for sufferers comes from research in Canada and Australia, where it has been discovered that Manuka honey can conquer these biofilm fortresses. Substances in the honey break the mucus shell and prevent communication and cell division in the bacteria, after which the bacteria succumb to the honey's antimicrobial agents. They also don't get a chance to develop resistance to the honey, as it is a very

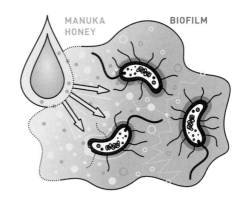

complex, synergistic cocktail of active ingredients and not a single substance, as is the case with antibiotics.

Insertion with cotton buds

You can also introduce the honey into the nose using normal cotton buds, although some of the precious honey will always remain in the absorbent cotton. I have previously tried intra- or endonasal reflex therapy with extra-long cotton swabs, with which you can reach deep into the sinuses, using a mixture of Manuka honey and Manuka oil. This method can be very effective, but you should consult a healthcare professional before trying it.

USAGE TIP

For effective nasal rinses, practice makes perfect. Before you flood your nose with the precious honey mixture, you should perform a basic cleansing with lukewarm, slightly salted water. You can also practice in advance with plain water how best to run the honey solution into your nose, distribute it throughout the nose and let it stay there as long as possible. To do this, hold one nostril closed and adjust your head position to achieve the desired effect. Try it first with a teaspoon of Manuka honey MGO100+ in a glass (about 150 ml) of warm water. You can use a commercial nasal douche to introduce the mixture in a comfortable and controlled way. Inflamed and sore mucous membranes may cause initially some pain. This is unpleasant, but should subside significantly once the honey's anti-inflammatory agents have soothed the sore areas. After that, you can increase the concentration of the solution and the MGO value to 250+.

Inhalation

Another way to get the honey into every corner of the sinuses is inhalation. To do this, you could use an ultrasonic nebulizer with a mask. The fine mist of honey is easy to inhale and coats the mucous membranes in the respiratory tract.

However, you might want to try good old-fashioned steam inhalation. You can easily do this twice for five to ten minutes, preferably just before going to bed.

USAGE TIP

Dissolve one heaped teaspoon of Manuka honey (MGO 250+) in a small bowl of boiled hot water. Sit comfortably in front of it and bring your head as close over the bowl as you can bear. You should drape a towel over your head and the bowl so that as little as possible of the precious honey vapour escapes. The most important thing is to inhale deeply, preferably through the nose. As the water cools down, you can lean closer towards the vapour source.

You can enhance the effect with a few drops of Manuka oil. By inhaling, you ensure that the active substances in the honey almost automatically reach the entire respiratory tract, including the lungs, or at least the bronchial tubes. Complementary oral ingestion of the honey is highly recommended.

CASE STUDY

A woman who suffered for many years from allergies and shortness of breath (with a tendency to COPD) told me that inhaling with Manuka honey gave her great relief after just a few sessions. She even found a use for the cooled honey water: she gave it to her dogs to drink, who really enjoyed it.

Throat and airway

We are now no longer in the nose and sinuses, but one level below (many pathogens move between levels). When we have a cold, viruses and bacteria are not content to stay in the nose. They also try to colonise other areas of the body. As they migrate, they leave us with inflamed mucous membranes in the throat, the pharynx and the bronchial tubes. Our immune system reacts with fever, sneezing and coughing.

Support your body with Manuka honey. In addition to inhaling it as a vapour, let small amounts of honey glide down your throat so that it coats the mucous membranes.

DID YOU KNOW?

In some British hospitals, Manuka honey is given to cancer patients to accompany chemotherapy and radiotherapy to prevent or treat the mucositis (inflammation of the mucous membranes) that usually occurs as a side effect of such aggressive treatment.

Since the beginning of 2020, we have seen the world brought to its knees by a previously unknown pathogen. I have been asked several times whether Manuka honey can offer any protection against corona virus. Observations so far suggest that people with a strong immune system can recover from Covid-19 relatively quickly and easily. Honey can help with that.

A special characteristic of the virus is that it first begins to multiply in the upper throat area before reaching the lungs, where the most severe symptoms are triggered. As we have seen, honey treatment for the lungs is difficult, but a precautionary covering of the pharyngeal mucous membranes with a honey film could help prevent colonisation by the virus. However, Manuka honey also has a beneficial effect under far less dramatic circumstances.

Oesophagus

There shouldn't be a crumb to eat in the lungs, thus the epiglottis prevents food from getting into the windpipe. It directs gases into the airway and solids and liquids into the oesophagus. But very rarely, something goes wrong. Air in the stomach is no big deal, but food getting sent down into the lungs immediately calls all the body's emergency responders

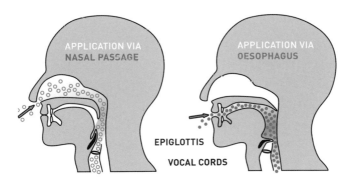

APPLICATION VIA NASAL PASSAGE

APPLICATION VIA OESOPHAGUS

EPIGLOTTIS

VOCAL CORDS

into action. If we inhale solids or liquids, we always react with an unstoppable coughing fit until the intruder is expelled. In this sensitive area, the larynx and vocal cords can benefit from the lubricating function of Manuka.

USAGE TIP

To support the larynx and vocal cords, take Manuka honey in the morning on an empty stomach and repeat in the evening. Seek medical advice and avoid harmful substances and activities.

The oesophagus is a forgiving hero. Hot, cold, coarse, spicy, sour – it swallows it all without protests or strikes. However, it has its limits, namely alcohol, drugs and other acidic irritants. Some of us suffer from inflammation of the oesophagus (oesophagitis). If there is a constant reflux of acidic stomach content at the entrance to the stomach, this inflammation is called reflux oesophagitis. Here too, the healing influence of Manuka honey has been proven many times.

Stomach ...

This also applies to our digestive tract. Invigorating food quickly becomes irritating if it gives you an irritable stomach or colon. Modern medicine often attributes such ailments to the mental state. If you are plagued by alternating gut pain, diarrhoea and constipation, would it be reassuring to be told that they have a psychological cause? This assumption has long been applied to chronic gastritis (inflammation of the mucous membrane of the stomach) and to stomach and duodenal ulcers. But in the mid-1980s, a strain of bacteria was discovered that was able to survive in the caustic-acidic environment of the stomach: helicobacter pylori.

If hydrochloric acid and the digestive enzyme pepsin have no effect on this bacterium and antibiotics work only temporarily, how is it that Manuka honey can provide relief and healing? Researchers at TU Dresden, who discovered the active ingredient methylglyoxal (MGO), did not rest before they found the answer to this question. In 2017, they discovered that the bacteria protect themselves from acid, pepsin and other attackers with an ammonia shell, which they make from urea using the enzyme urease.

If you take away one of these components, the bacteria lose their ability to protect themselves. Prof Henle's team managed to prove that the MGO and DHA contained in Manuka honey act as urease inhibitors. Without its protective ammonia coat, helicobacter can be attacked by gastric acid, pepsin and, of course, by the antimicrobial effect of the honey. Armed with this knowledge, we should stop treating stomach and intestinal diseases caused by helicobacter pylori with antibiotics, which don't offer a sustainable solution and do cause lasting damage to our intestinal flora. Instead, the remedy of first choice should be Manuka honey. When treating the stomach with Manuka honey MGO400+ or higher, you should try to visualise the inner path the honey will follow.

USAGE TIP

A proven method of spreading the honey over the entire stomach lining, and thus getting it into every part of the stomach, is the classic German "Rollkur" (rolling cure). To do this, take a tablespoon of Manuka honey and lie down. Imagine a film of honey covering the entire stomach lining, while you encourage this by turning your body into different horizontal positions (on your back, left side, belly, right side).

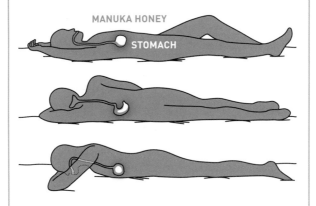

MANUKA HONEY

STOMACH

This treatment is most effective in the morning and on an empty stomach and should be repeated just before bedtime. Taking honey in the evening can also help with sleep disorders as it ensures a sufficient fuel supply for the brain, which in turn doesn't keep us awake half the night with its endless anxiety-driven attempts to refuel.

... and gut

The further we go into the intestine to provide treatment with Manuka honey, the less the effect of the honey can be attributed exclusively to the methylglyoxal.

In this respect, the Dresden researchers made another interesting discovery. MGO is metabolised in the small intestine. However, the resulting metabolites – such as lactic acid – also seem to have an antimicrobial, and thus positive effect on our intestinal flora.

MGO metabolites and other honey elements must therefore be responsible for the antimicrobial and anti-inflammatory effect of the honey in the large intestine and even in the internal organs.

Anecdotal evidence even suggests that inflammatory diseases of the colon such as ulcerative colitis or Crohn's disease can be treated with Manuka honey. A doctor who was due to undergo surgery for inflammation of the intestinal wall (diverticulitis) cancelled the scheduled operation because he managed to get the problem under control with Manuka honey.

USAGE TIP

The procedure for treating infections and inflammations in the stomach is also recommended for the gut. Take at least one teaspoon of MGO400+ between meals, preferably early in the morning and last thing at night. In order to benefit from the entire spectrum of Manuka honey's benefits, you could supplement your oral intake with enemas of honey solution. As with the nasal rinsing already described, a pre-rinse with warm water or chamomile tea would be advisable. Then dissolve one tablespoon of MGO250+ in up to half a litre of warm water and inject it slowly into the large intestine using an enema or irrigator and keep it there for as long as possible. The amount can of course be adjusted. If there is a lot of liquid, the pressure on the sphincter muscle naturally increases and we can only retain the honey solution for a short time.

Internal organs

Strictly speaking, the stomach and intestines are not internal organs. The entire digestive tract is essentially a pipeline that, apart from a few valves and closures, is basically open at the top and bottom. This is not the case with internal organs such as the liver, kidneys, bladder and prostate.

Liver

"The liver grows with its tasks." The largest gland in the body plays a crucial and diverse role. On the one hand, it serves as a storage organ. It stores fructose and releases it again when needed. This is one reason why diabetics tolerate honey better than other sugars. The liver is also an important detoxifying organ and helps keep toxins at bay. A decisive factor in drug research is the first-pass effect, which refers to the metabolisation of orally ingested substances by the liver. The effect of the drug is weakened or strengthened by this metabolization, and the dosage must therefore be increased or decreased accordingly. If the active substances of honey are to reach their targets after their passage through the liver, it is a good idea to take this effect into account when determining the amount of honey to be taken.

USAGE TIP

One recipe that can help the liver recover includes two essential bee products: honey and pollen. The latter contains all the essential amino acids, i.e. protein building blocks that our body has to import because it doesn't produce them itself. The liver can improvise here and convert existing protein into amino acids, but if we ingest the protein, the liver doesn't have to do this work and can use its energies elsewhere.

To support the liver, mix one tablespoon of pollen and one teaspoon of Manuka honey MGO250+ or MGO400+ into 150 g of natural yoghurt. Give the pollen about 15 to 30 minutes to soften and stir everything thoroughly again. You can take this power mixture for several weeks or even months. Ideally, you simply substitute it for breakfast or dinner (In Germany, people eat a warm lunch).

In order not to tax this amazing organ excessively, we should limit our intake of stimulants such as alcohol. Another function of the liver is its ability to convert the amino acids (protein building blocks) absorbed from food in such a way that they can be turned into the body's own proteins (catalysis or transamination).

Kidneys, bladder and prostate

As the scope of this book is limited, I cannot go into detail about every part of the body. Most things can be deduced from other descriptions, and you simply have to try some things for yourself. There's not much you can do wrong, except not to try Manuka honey at all.

USAGE TIP

For the treatment of kidney, bladder or prostate infections, you can use Manuka honey in two ways. One is to take pure Manuka honey MGO400+, at least one teaspoon two to three times a day, which you keep in your mouth for as long as possible before swallowing. The salivation process initiates carbohydrate digestion in the mouth, and the valuable elements of the honey get absorbed in the mouth without having to survive the acidic environment of the stomach.

The second way is to combine the honey with green tea (synergy effects). You can drink 1.5 to 2 litres of green tea (ideally organic) per day with one teaspoon of Manuka honey MGO400+ per cup. Allow the hot tea to cool slightly before stirring in the honey. Boiling-hot water extracts more nutrients from the tea. Manuka honey is not as sensitive as other honeys and can be heated above 40°C, but not above 70°C. A friend of mine and Manuka dealer has cured two bouts of prostatitis with this mixture – although he wasn't exactly sparing with the honey.

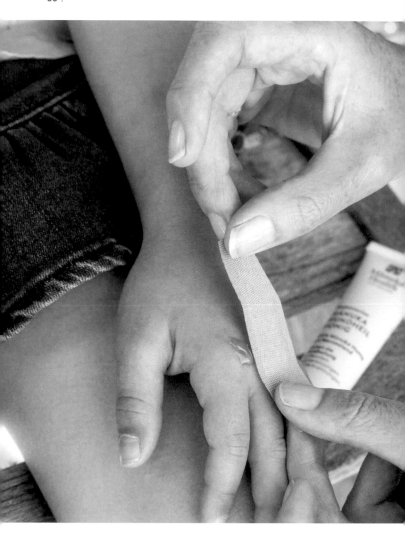

APPLYING MANUKA – THE HONEY AS TREATMENT

APPLYING MANUKA – THE HONEY AS TREATMENT

Our skin

It is often said that our largest organ is the skin, but if you were to smooth out all the crevices of our intestines, it would be much larger than the skin. Nevertheless, it is certainly true that the skin is the largest sense organ, protecting us from dangers such as heat and cold as well as forming a barrier against pathogens.

Our skin defies wind and rain, but also enjoys refreshing coolness, cosy warmth and tender touch. It is home to an unimaginably large army of microorganisms, most of which are benevolent and useful to us. Any damage to this protective cover requires immediate repair.

Damage can be caused by internal or external factors. Whatever the cause, we can support our body in its efforts to restore a healthy normal state by using Manuka honey internally and externally.

Wounds

The use of Manuka honey to treat wounds is probably the most common application of this precious
resource worldwide and one of the most studied.
It helps that a wound is also a clearly defined area
of application that can be easily targeted and mon-
itored.

Especially in chronically infected wounds, honey
can demonstrate the entire range of its healing
effects. It doesn't matter whether the bacteria are
antibiotic-resistant or not. The honey will support
the skin's healing processes and defences.

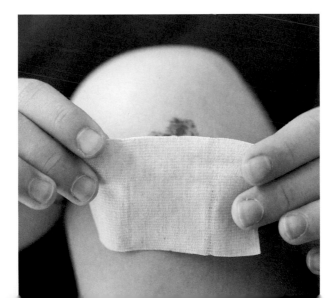

How does the honey work on the wound?

The following summarises the diversity and inter-connectedness of Manuka honey's various clinical effects:

Osmotic

Due to its high sugar content, honey draws water. Water gets extracted from bacteria, whilst water retention is relieved. For wounds, it creates a moist environment, which supports the regrowth of skin cells and tissue. It also helps defence cells to dispose of waste from the wound area.

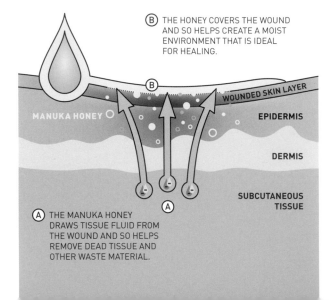

(B) THE HONEY COVERS THE WOUND AND SO HELPS CREATE A MOIST ENVIRONMENT THAT IS IDEAL FOR HEALING.

WOUNDED SKIN LAYER

MANUKA HONEY

EPIDERMIS

DERMIS

SUBCUTANEOUS TISSUE

(A) THE MANUKA HONEY DRAWS TISSUE FLUID FROM THE WOUND AND SO HELPS REMOVE DEAD TISSUE AND OTHER WASTE MATERIAL.

Antimicrobial

The wound becomes sterile. Bacteria as well as fungi and viruses disappear, even if they are coated in biofilms. This is a basic requirement for a smooth healing process.

Anti-inflammatory

Excessive immune reactions are hindered so that the healing process can do its magic.

Does not stick to the wound

Disturbance of the granulation layer (young regrowing cell tissue) is avoided. A change of dressing usually causes less pain, and the wound environment is less irritated.

Stimulating the immune system

Thanks to the osmotic effect, the wound is well managed and disposes of dead, often foul-smelling material.

Probiotic

The wound area is directly supplied with nutrients and vital substances, thus accelerating the healing process.

Minimal keloid formation (scarring)

Fresh tissue grows from the depths and the edges of the wound, so that the wound heals more than just superficially, and the formation of raised and numb scars is avoided.

Manuka honey is therefore clearly superior to many conventional wound remedies. This list covers just some of the aspects of Manuka's diverse effects and functions.

USAGE TIP

For wound treatment, MGO100+ is usually sufficient. Apply enough honey to a compress suitable for the size of the wound so that the wound is completely filled and the edges of the wound are covered.

Put the honey side of the compress on the wound and bandage well. If the wound discharges heavily, the dressing may need to be changed several times a day. Later, you can leave the dressing on the wound for two to three days.

The body's own secretions (pus and other fluids) may cause the wound to stick to the dressing. You should change the dressing frequently, especially at the beginning of the treatment.

Manuka honey and the methylglyoxal it contains are effective over a long period of time, even under a thick dressing. Just don't let the honey dry out completely.

A German man told me that after more than two years of unsuccessful medical interventions, including twenty operations, his hip operation scar, which had a hospital-acquired infection, had finally closed after only four weeks of treatment with Manuka honey.

Fresh wounds treated immediately with Manuka honey don't get infected or enflamed. The healing is fast and sustained.

CASE STUDY

One of my friends likes to 'give people the finger' – not to insult them but to share his Manuka experience with them. During a holiday in Italy, a door of his camper van crushed the tip of his middle finger so badly that the bone was exposed. Although his wife urged him to get "proper" wound care with stitches, disinfection and bandaging at the hospital, he bandaged the wound himself with Manuka.

Only when he returned home did he have his finger examined by a doctor, who immediately wanted to know who had treated the wound so well. "I did it myself with honey," my friend replied. "With Manuka?" the doctor asked and added, "My father also swears by it." The friend also likes to remark that the dressing material was more expensive than the honey he used, the cost of which he puts at less than € 2.

Needless to say, I don't want to discourage you from going to the doctor if you have a serious injury, but I also don't believe in the trivialising and disenfranchising advice that only allows you to treat yourself with honey for harmless skin abrasions. In any event, the Manuka honey dressing is entirely suitable as an initial treatment. Otherwise, you should proceed as per the usage tip for burns on p. 60.

Chronically infected wounds such as leg ulcers, diabetic foot syndrome or decubitus ulcers can all be treated successfully with Manuka honey. If you are uncomfortable with the idea of using edible honey therapeutically, you can instead use a wound-healing Manuka honey registered as a medical product and marketed by a reputable provider.

Burns

Burns range in severity from slight, superficial scalds to deep destruction of the skin. This type of injury can leave us completely defenceless by removing the barrier against pathogens.

If the burn is treated with honey, there is a good chance that scarring will be limited. Strict adherence to hygiene is essential. Large, severe burns pose a serious risk and require professional medical attention.

USAGE TIP

For extensive and serious burns, seek immediate medical attention and take a jar of Manuka Honey MGO100+ or some Manuka wound-healing honey with you if necessary. Share your knowledge of honey and its fantastic properties with your healthcare professional, but don't abdicate responsibility for your health. You can treat less severe, smaller burns yourself by applying Manuka honey to sterile dressing material, carefully applying it to the burnt area and gently bandaging it.

In the case of burns, immediate use of honey can play a vital protective role. In the absence of our natural acidic protective coating, honey can act as a substitute and prevent pathogenic bacteria from getting in to the wound. After an initial burning sensation, a cooling and pain-relieving effect soon sets in.

Inflammatory skin diseases

In Chinese medicine, each organ and disease symptom is considered in light of whole-body energy. The aim is not only to treat symptoms but to find their cause and restore balance. Pathological skin symptoms are therefore often attributed to poor intestinal health.

This philosophy aims at restoring gut health and avoiding foods that, due to latent intolerance, keep the gut's immune system unnecessarily busy. To compensate for its energy deficiency, the gut then taxes its partner organs, the lungs and the skin.

It is said that the ancient Chinese doctors were paid to keep their patients healthy rather than simply treat them when they got ill. A concept worthy of emulation, in my opinion, and which is also reflected in the English saying, "An ounce of prevention is better than a pound of cure". A total maintenance programme would need to be carefully thought out in advance, but there is no reason why external symptoms can't be treated immediately.

In case of acne, both the antibacterial and the anti-inflammatory properties of Manuka honey are effective. In case of neurodermatitis or psoriasis, the anti-inflammatory and antioxidant, as well as the moisturising and nourishing effects of honey can contribute to the regeneration of the skin and thus to overall wellbeing.

USAGE TIP
Wash the skin and hands and apply Manuka Honey MGO100+ in a thin layer. Leave the honey on for at least half an hour. Skincare professionals recommend applying a warm, damp cloth over the honey. This also helps to open the pores and allows the honey to be better absorbed. Of course, you can only do this routine when you're not busy. A good remedy for in-between times would be Manuka oil mixed with a carrier oil of

your choice. You can apply this over a large area and massage it in. It is absorbed well and is not sticky like honey. Ready-made mixtures may use almond, macadamia or calendula oil, but olive or hemp oil could also be used. For years, I have been making an ointment from olive and avocado oil, beeswax, manuka honey, manuka oil and alcohol-free propolis solution. My daughter swears by it as a lip balm and as a remedy for skincare and sunburn. There are also highly recommended ready-made products from the largest supplier of Manuka honey on the German market.

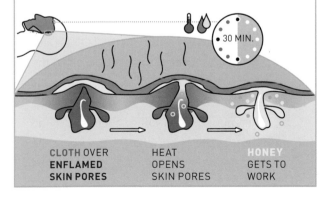

30 MIN.

CLOTH OVER
ENFLAMED
SKIN PORES

HEAT
OPENS
SKIN PORES

HONEY
GETS TO
WORK

Oral herpes

Oral herpes can be a persistent and distressing condition. The viruses that cause it are unfortunately opportunists that are hard to get rid of. They live deep inside us and take advantage of every opportunity, when our defences are weakened or we are otherwise stressed, to break out again. Don't worry! Manuka honey is there to save you!

USAGE TIP

Applying Manuka honey MGO100+ or stronger at the first sign of an outbreak can prevent it from progressing. Applying the honey to already fully developed herpes blisters also speeds up the healing process. The frequency of outbreaks will also decrease. Propolis tincture in combination or in alternation with honey has also proven to be effective.

Inflammation of the eyes

Honey was used in ancient times as an eye medicine. An Egyptian doctor I know from apitherapy congresses (apitherapy = medical use of bee products) does not only treat diabetics with intravenous honey injections, but also the most severe eye infections. I myself have successfully treated a stye (staphylococcus infection of various glands in the eye) with Manuka. It certainly takes some willpower, but it is worth it.

USAGE TIP

To treat a stye, apply a little Manuka honey to the lower eyelid with a clean finger and spread it with the blink of an eye. There will be a strong burning sensation at first, but this is immediately stopped by heavy watering in the eye. Afterwards, you will be left with a fresh and clean feeling. To ensure that the bacteria do not return elsewhere, the procedure should be repeated several times a day and continued even after the stye has disappeared. The redness of the sclerae (the white around thepupils) will quickly subside.

> The eye tissue (the conjunctiva) will probably experience increased blood flow which is certainly not wrong. Overnight the effect can be enhanced by applying Manuka honey MGO100+ or stronger to the closed eye using a cotton pad and fixing it with a blindfold. The same procedure can be applied to other infectious and inflammatory eye conditions. And remember, Manuka honey has an antimicrobial effect, i.e. against bacteria as well as against fungi and viruses.

Fungal infections

To many of us, the fact that Manuka honey is effective against fungi is not immediately obvious; yeast fungi in particular have a great affinity for sugar and honey consists mainly of various sugars. However, with the sugar from Manuka honey, the fungi also absorb methylglyoxal, which is just as bad for them as it is for other bacterial and viral pathogens. The honey supports our microbiome (useful bacteria that protect us). This creates a hostile environment for fungal parasites. Direct contact with the antimicrobial agents in honey does the rest.

Studies have shown that bees also fight intestinal fungi with honey. Valuable lactic acid bacteria (bifidobacteria and lactobacilli), on the other hand, are nurtured and cared for by them.

USAGE TIP

Women with a vaginal yeast infection (vaginal mycosis) have had very good experiences with Manuka honey-soaked tampons (MGO250+ or stronger), which can quickly put an end to this annoying condition. I also recommend this procedure for bladder infections, so that the bacteria are not replenished through the urethra. In case of fungal infections, I recommend an alcohol-free propolis solution in combination or in alternation with honey. Propolis is made by bees from the resins of plants that use it to protect themselves from fungal infections.

Manuka honey for pets

One of the first anecdotes about Manuka honey I heard many years ago was that beekeeping dairy farmers in New Zealand mixed the honey, which hardly anyone wanted to buy a few decades ago, into their cows' feed. The cows were said to be much healthier and more resistant to diseases as a result. Although I have not yet been able to find the original source of this statement, I'm sure it is true. After all, there are many pet owners, vets and animal healers who have been able to achieve very good results with Manuka honey given to dogs, cats and horses.

The actual honey producers, the bees themselves, use their products primarily to maintain their own health. The antimicrobial effect of honey works against a multitude of pathogens, regardless of whether they are humans or animals.

Manuka honey is also an excellent remedy in veterinary wound care, ensuring rapid healing. The animal may try to lick the sweet-tasting honey off, but the honey would still work internally. However,

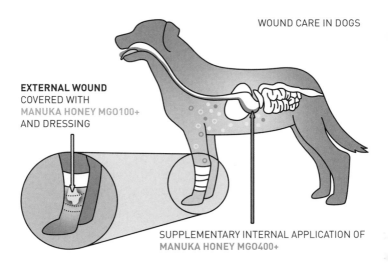

WOUND CARE IN DOGS

EXTERNAL WOUND
COVERED WITH
MANUKA HONEY MGO100+
AND DRESSING

SUPPLEMENTARY INTERNAL APPLICATION OF
MANUKA HONEY MGO400+

to ensure undisturbed wound healing, you should offer your pet the honey directly for licking and take measures to keep its tongue away from the wound.

Of course, Manuka Honey can also be used to treat infections and inflammations in your pet's mouth and digestive tract. You probably don't need to mix the honey into the food or drinking water. Many animals like it pure because they like the taste, and they instinctively know that it is good for them.

Manuka oil

Like honey, Manuka oil comes from the Manuka plant (leptospermum scoparium). However, it is not extracted by bees from the flower nectar, but by humans from the leaves through steam distillation. Some call it the "real" tea tree oil, especially since Captain James Cook gave the Manuka bush the name tea tree before he came to Australia. Compared to Australian tea tree oil from the local tea tree (melaleuca alternifolia), Manuka oil has a much stronger antimicrobial effect, although it is less irritating as it contains far less cineole, which can also lead to irritation of the skin and stomach, although it provides a certain therapeutic benefit (it has an expectorant and cooling effect in eucalyptus oil).

Both Manuka oil and Manuka honey contain the phytotherapeutic active ingredients of the Manuka plant in different proportions. The pure oil can be used against warts, athlete's foot and nail fungus. For extensive inflammation of the skin, it can be used in a carrier oil mixture at a ratio of 2:100. A ready-mixed oil is also available from specialist retailers.

MANUKA PIONEERS IN GERMANY

Reinhard Kuhfuß and
Prof. Dr. Dr. Thomas Henle

MANUKA PIONEERS IN GERMANY

Reinhard Kuhfuß

When I was researching my first honey book in 2005/2006, I came across Manuka honey on the Internet. The importer who immediately caught my eye was the German company Neuseelandhaus (founded 1996). They brought Manuka honey to national attention and were committed to standardised quality tests. I sent them an email asking for more information. Company founder and managing director Reinhard Kuhfuß called me and told me that he had been looking for an author who could write about Manuka honey for some time. With his help I wrote a separate chapter on Manuka and a press release on decoding the Unique Manuka Factor (UMF, see p. 16). While I was still writing The Healing Power of Honey, Manuka helped me enormously. I was able to avert incipient tendonitis by applying honey compresses and continued writing pain-free.

Prof. Dr. Dr. Thomas Henle

The second pioneer is the man who discovered methylglyoxal (MGO) in Manuka honey, Prof Thomas Henle of TU Dresden (Chair of Food Chemistry) (for an explanation of MGO, see p. 16). He had previously ordered the honey for his research at Neuseeland-haus.

His 2006 press release about the discovery of the central active ingredient in Manuka honey paved the way for the honey's worldwide recognition and ultimately brought the two pioneers together.

One of the largest producers of Manuka honey in New Zealand recognised the value of this discovery and was the first to use the university's method of measuring MGO to determine the honey's potency.

Since then, the MGO value of each honey has been measured using this method and is stated on the honey jar. Everyone has probably seen the distinctive brown jars with blue lids and labels and the red double honeycomb.

Reinhard Kuhfuß is for me the undisputed Manuka pioneer in Germany and has always been an enthusiastic user of, and ambassador for, this New Zealand jewel.

Since his ground-breaking discovery, Professor Henle has constantly researched the diverse effects of Manuka honey and continues to surprise us with new discoveries.

Both Manuka pioneers still communicate on the subject today and inspire each other with their practical and scientific findings.

A - Z OF USES

A - Z OF USES

Even though Manuka honey is sometimes perceived as a panacea or magic remedy, if you have a serious health problem, you should still consult a doctor or alternative healthcare practitioner about your treatment. Always apply the honey specifically to the place where it is intended to work (e.g. to an inflammation or where invading bacteria have caused an infection). However, judging by the numerous success stories, it also seems very likely that Manuka honey can work systemically in the bloodstream. The extent to which the honey simply stimulates the immune system (i.e. helps the body to help itself) is irrelevant. The following alphabetical list of uses is not intended to be exhaustive but simply to provide an overview of the way the honey can work.

A

Abscess | Apply Manuka honey MGO100+ or stronger directly into and onto the abscess and bandage. Consult a doctor. Check regularly.

Acne | Apply Manuka honey MGO100+ to the affected areas and cover. Best applied at home and overnight (see also usage tip on p. 62 in the chapter on inflammatory skin diseases chapter).

Allergies | Depending on the cause and symptoms, apply Manuka honey MGO100+ externally to inflamed skin, and MGO400+ internally to stabilise the immune system. Test your reaction with small amounts first.

Aphthae (mouth ulcer) | Apply small amounts of Manuka honey MGO250+ directly to the affected area of the mouth or gums and keep it in the mouth for as long as possible. Alternating or mixing treatment with propolis tincture increases efficacy.

Arthritis | Massage approximately ½ teaspoon of Manuka honey MGO100+ or stronger into the skin around the affected joint in circular movements. Then remove the honey in plucking movements with the fingers or rocking movements with the whole palm of the hand until the gum-like mass has all stuck to your hand and none remains on the skin. Wash the hand with lukewarm water. Apply new honey to the joint and bandage it, preferably with a large plaster. You can also do this without the honey massage. Taking Manuka honey and other bee products such as propolis and flower pollen at the same time can enhance the treatment internally.

Asthma | Take regular steam baths with Manuka honey MGO250+ and take small amounts orally throughout the day. In the evening, insert the honey into both nostrils and apply to the chest in the area of the bronchial tubes and cover loosely with a cotton cloth, foil or other type of wrap.

Athlete's foot | Mix Manuka honey MGO100+ with propolis tincture, apply to the affected areas and dress. For nail fungus, first roughen the nail, drizzle undiluted Manuka oil onto it and allow to absorb, then combine with the honey-propolis mixture.

B

Bed sores | See → Pressure sores

Bladder infection | Drink one to two litres of green tea with one teaspoon of Manuka honey MGO400+ per cup throughout the day. Women can additionally counteract a bladder infection caused by bacteria from the ureters by inserting a honey-soaked tampon, possibly mixed with five to ten drops of alcohol-free propolis solution.

Bronchitis | Let small amounts of Manuka Honey MGO250+ dissolve in the mouth throughout the day. Stir a teaspoon of the honey into 'cough tea' (thyme, coltsfoot, ribwort, etc.) and drink in small sips. You can also make a syrup with the fresh herbs or with grated horseradish or onions, which should be chopped into small pieces, crushed and stirred into the honey. Leave to infuse overnight and take by the teaspoonful as required. The following mixture is also recommended: dissolve a tablespoon of Manuka honey in a glass of warm water and add a strong dash of apple cider vinegar and drink immediately in sips. See also → Asthma

Burns | Consult a doctor and avoid the infection of the wound. For minor burns, apply Manuka honey MGO100+ to sterile dressing material and carefully apply to burnt area. Gently dress. Initially change the dressing several times a day.

C

Cancer | Manuka honey and propolis have anti-carcinogenic properties. As an accompanying treatment to conventional cancer therapy, they may enhance the efficacy of treatment and reduce or prevent unpleasant side-effects.

Candida albicans (yeast infection) | In addition to a fungal diet, i.e. largely avoiding carbohydrates, try a teaspoon of Manuka honey MGO400+ and 10 drops of propolis tincture three times a day. For vaginal mycosis (vaginal yeast infection), inserting a honey-soaked tampon often helps. See also → Bladder infection

Caries (tooth decay) | Caused by bacteria and promoted by an imbalance of mouth flora (dysbiosis). Manuka honey helps counteract pathological bacteria and promote healthy bacteria. I use a toothpaste that contains Manuka honey MGO400+, propolis and Manuka oil. Lubricating the mouth with Manuka honey and propolis tincture two to three times a day ensures a healthy oral environment. Sugar normally promotes the formation of caries bacteria, but the methylglyoxal in combination with the sugar is toxic to such offenders.

Conjunctivitis | See → Eye inflammation

Corneal inflammation (keratitis) | See → Eye inflammation

Cough | See → Bronchitis

Couperosis (erysipelas, rosacea) | This is caused not only by a disturbed immune system and excessive nerve and vascular reactions, but also by microbial triggers such as the demodex mite. Spicy food, alcohol and sudden changes in temperature aggravate the redness, which occurs mainly on the face. Due to its antimicrobial effect, which works against secondary bacterial infections but also possibly against the mites directly, as well as its anti-inflammatory properties, Manuka honey is a recommended treatment. Apply Manuka honey MGO100+ to the affected areas. Be patient and avoid physical and mental stressors. See also → Acne → Neurodermatitis

Crohn's disease | Can occur in the entire digestive tract from the oral cavity to the anus, but usually in the last part of the small intestine and passing into the colon. See also → Ulcerative colitis → Helicobacter pylori → Diarrhoea

Cystitis | See → Bladder infection

D

Depression | This common side effect of chronic illnesses may improve with recovery from underlying illness treated with honey and other bee products. Manuka honey MGO250+ mixed with flower pollen and royal jelly can bring about a significant mood lift. However, it is not a substitute for professional help and support from those closest to you.

Diabetic foot syndrome | Cover the affected area generously with Manuka honey MGO100+ and a bandage. Initially dressings should be changed daily, possibly even several times a day. Intervals can be extended as healing progresses, but the dressing should not be allowed to dry out completely, as it will then stick to the wound and cause pain and injury to the tissue when removed. Adhesion is always caused by fluid from the wound, never by the honey.

Diarrhoea | Swallow a teaspoon of Manuka honey MGO400+ several times a day. Its selective antibiotic effect restores balance in the intestinal flora. In case of prolonged diarrhoea, lost water and electrolytes need to be replaced. Take 2 tablespoons of honey and 1 level teaspoon of salt dissolved in 1 litre of warm water. Drink quickly.

Diverticulitis (diverticulosis) | Diverticula = protrusions of the gut lining that have become inflamed.

Diet should be rich in fibre, but not too coarse or long-fibred. Drink plenty of water. A doctor who suffered from this condition reported that he was able to cancel a scheduled operation by taking Manuka honey. See also → Ulcerative colitis

Duodenal ulcers | See → Helicobacter pylori

E

Eye inflammation | Apply a small amount of Manuka honey MGO100+, possibly stronger, to the lower eyelid with your clean little finger and spread over the eyeball by blinking. Warning: you may experience a temporary but strong burning sensation, redness and eye-watering. You can also apply the honey to the closed eye, especially at night, using a cotton pad coated with the honey and a blindfold. Continue treatment, even after improvement, until the inflammation has healed (see also the usage tip on p. 65 in the chapter on eye inflammation).

Eczema, also atopic eczema (neurodermatitis) | Apply Manuka honey MGO100+ directly to the affected areas and bandage if necessary. Avoid allergens. See also → Allergies → Neurodermatitis

F

Flu, influenza infections, viral flu | As a preventive measure, take one teaspoon of Manuka honey MGO100+ three times a day. In the acute stage, you should use a stronger Manuka honey and let 1 g of royal jelly melt slowly in your mouth. Also apply the honey to the nose. Avoid pork, as flu viruses spend the summer in pigs. This is a valuable tip from Dr Reckeweg that I have been following for about 40 years and I have never had the flu again.

G

Gastritis | Avoid spicy food, acids, alcohol and stress. See → Helicobacter pylori

Genital herpes | Proceed as for → Oral herpes, use non-alcoholic propolis solution. Same pathogen, different entry site.

Gingivitis (inflammation of the gums) | Apply Manuka Honey MGO250+ directly to the inflamed gums. Keep in the mouth for as long as possible. The honey will draw a lot of saliva. Rinse your gums with the saliva/honey mixture. Propolis tincture also works well. See also → Aphthae

H

Hay fever, pollen allergy | Hyposensitisation with honey from the region. See also → Allergies

Haemorrhoids | These varicose veins at the anus tend to bleed, are often painful and can cause severe itching. Suppositories made of beeswax, or Manuka honey MGO250+ and propolis, or a honey-soaked tampon can counteract infections and relieve symptoms. It is also important to support and treat your liver. Stirring pollen into honey is also recommended.

Heartburn (oesophagitis due to gastric acid reflux) | One teaspoon of Manuka honey MGO250+ or stronger three times a day. Swallow quickly and lie down. Avoid acid-forming foods. See also → Mucositis

Helicobacter pylori | This bacterium survives the acid inferno in our stomach and is at least partly responsible for gastritis (inflammation of the stomach lining), stomach ulcers and duodenal ulcers. Take a generous teaspoon of Manuka Honey MGO400+ immediately after getting up and right before going to bed, swallow it quickly and lie down. Change your lying position several times in the manner of a classic "Rollkur" (rolling cure). If you can, do the same exercise again before lunch. And be persistent; helicobacter is too.

Herpes labialis | See → Oral herpes

Herpes zoster | See → Shingles

Hordeolum (styes) | See → Eye inflammation

Hospital bacteria | See → Wounds

I

Intestinal inflammation | See → Ulcerative colitis → Diverticulitis → Helicobacter pylori → Crohn's disease

K

Keratitis (corneal inflammation) | See → Eye inflammation

L

Laryngitis | Stress-related inflammation of the larynx caused by viral infection, excessive talking, smoking, dry air, gastric reflux, obstructed nasal breathing, etc. Swallow Manuka honey MGO250+ (possibly lying on the stomach) in small amounts, alternating or combining with propolis tincture, if necessary. A teaspoon of honey in a cup of sage tea is also recommended. Drink several times a day in small sips. Avoid harmful factors and activities. In case of chronic laryngitis, consult a doctor. See also → Sore throat

Leg ulcers (ulcus cruris) | Fill and dress the ulcer with Manuka honey MGO100+. Initially change the dressing several times a day if necessary and rinse with saline solution. Seek medical attention. See also → Diabetic foot syndrome and → Pressure sores

Lyme disease | As a preventive measure, you can apply propolis tincture to the fresh tick bite and then bandage it with a Manuka honey patch. As already mentioned, no research has yet been done into the effectiveness of Manuka honey against Lyme disease, but anecdotal evidence suggests many sufferers have achieved to get back to a normal life, even after losing mobility, by taking one teaspoon of Manuka honey MGO400+ two to three times a day, in addition to other measures.

M

Mouth sores (aphthous stomatitis) | Sores caused by herpes infection in the entire oral cavity. See also → Aphthae → Oral herpes

Mucositis (inflammation of the mucous membranes) | Especially in the mouth, throat and oesophagus, often as a side effect of chemotherapy. Melt Manuka honey MGO250+ in the mouth as required and swallow slowly, thereby coating the affected mucous membranes. The osmotic, moisturising effect of the honey alone provides some relief. At the same time, pathogens and inflammation are reduced. See also → Aphthae → Gingivitis → Mouth sores → Sore throat

N

Nail fungus | See → Athlete's foot

Neurodermatitis (atopic eczema) | Apply Manuka Honey MGO100+ directly to the affected skin area and dress. Apply Manuka oil mixed with a skin-friendly carrier oil (1:50 mix, 2%). Tip: use Manuka honey at night and Manuka oil during the day. Avoid allergens. Ready-made mixtures are available from retailers.

O

Oesophagitis | See → Heartburn

Oral herpes, herpes simplex, cold sores | Use Manuka honey MGO100+ or stronger and/or propolis tincture. Apply directly to the herpes blisters or to the tense area you feel before the outbreak. Be prepared for such outbreaks, especially in times of stress. The honey or propolis treatment will lead to faster healing and fewer recurrences.

P

Pancreatitis (inflammation of the pancreas) | Avoid alcohol and refined sugar. Take one teaspoon of Manuka honey MGO400+ three times a day. For one of the three doses, mix the honey with one tablespoon of pollen and 150 g of yoghurt. Taking it while lying down can enhance efficacy.

Pharyngitis | See → Sore throat

Phlebitis | See → Venous inflammation

Periodontitis (serious inflammation of the gums) | Progression of the bacterial infection can be halted using Manuka honey MGO250+ and pro-polis tincture. See also → Gingivitis and other inflammations in the oral cavity

Pollen allergy | Hyposensitisation with honey from the region. See also → Allergies

Pressure sores | Apply Manuka Honey MGO100+ directly to the pressure ulcer, covering the entire damaged area beyond the edges. A skin-compatible film can be applied over the first layer of dressing, which is then covered with a cotton pad. Avoid permanent pressure on individual pressure points.

Prostatitis | Procedure as for → Bladder infection. Drink one to two litres of green tea with one teaspoon of Manuka honey MGO400+ per cup through-out the day.

Psoriasis | Apply Manuka honey MGO100+ to the affected areas and dress if necessary. Apitherapists recommend taking the honey and other bee products such as flower pollen, propolis and royal jelly at the same time. Many of them also treat psoriasis with bee venom. See also → Neurodermatitis

R

Rhinitis | Apply Manuka Honey MGO250+ to the nose and inhale deeply. Repeat several times a day. Honey does not dry out the nasal mucous membranes. See also → Rhinosinusitis

Rhinosinusitis (nasal sinusitis, also chronically maintained by biofilms) | Perform nasal irrigation with Manuka honey MGO250+ or stronger. Prior cleansing with saline solution is recommended. Then pour the honey, dissolved in warm water in a ratio of about 1:10, into a nasal douche vessel. Holding one nostril shut and using your tongue to stop the mixture going down your throat, let the mixture flow into the other nostril. Adjust your head position so that the solution can penetrate into the sinuses to take effect directly on the mucous membrane and to prevent it from draining away unused. Then, especially overnight, apply pure Manuka honey deep into the nose, possibly into the sinuses with longer cotton swabs. Inhale by breathing through the nose. If you use the honey while lying down, you can ensure it will be targeted at the affected areas. Give it a try and be persistent; biofilms are too.

Rosacea | See → Couperosis

S

Shingles (herpes zoster) | If you have ever had chicken pox, you carry the pathogen inside you. Taking Manuka honey and propolis prophylactically may prevent an outbreak. An application of Manuka honey MGO100+, possibly mixed with propolis tincture, can reduce the rash along the affected nerve pathways and the associated pain, as well as contain the spread of the viruses.

Sinusitis | See → Rhinosinusitis

Sore throat | Suck small amounts of Manuka Honey MGO250+ and let it slowly trickle down the throat. To do this, first put the honey on a spoon and, over a period of about fifteen minutes, lick the spoon several times as you would eat an ice cream. Time is more important than quantity. Simultaneous insertion of the honey into the nose helps to prevent the throat inflammation from being maintained by germs from the nasal and sinus areas.

Stomach ulcer (ulcus ventriculi) | See → Helico-bacter pylori

Stomatitis | Take small amounts of Manuka Honey MGO250+ in the mouth as required and keep them there for as long as possible. Salivate well and distribute throughout the oral cavity. See also → Aphthae→ Gingivitis → Mucositis → Caries

Styes (hordeolum) | See → Eye inflammation

T

Thrombophlebitis | See → Venous inflammation

Tick bite | See → Lyme disease

Tonsillitis | Use a brush to apply Manuka honey MGO250+ and/or propolis tincture directly onto the inflamed tonsils. Repeat several times a day. See also → Sore throat

Tooth decay | See → Caries

U

Ulcerative colitis | Chronic inflammatory bowel diseases are considered incurable. Nevertheless, try taking one teaspoon of Manuka honey MGO400+ three times a day with 10 drops of propolis tincture per teaspoon. You can do enemas with warm chamomile or sage tea in which you have dissolved the honey. Take about two tablespoons of Manuka honey MGO400+ in ½ litre of tea. Avoid stress.

Ulcus cruris | See → Leg ulcers

Ulcus ventriculi (stomach ulcer) | See → Helicobacter pylori

Urinary tract infection | See → Bladder infection

V

Venous inflammation (phlebitis – vascular inflammation caused by circulatory disorders, especially in the legs, "varicose veins") | Acute thrombosis and inflammation of surface leg veins is a precursor to venous leg ulcers. Thrombosis in the deep veins of the legs must be monitored by a doctor, as there is a risk of pulmonary embolism (blockage of the pulmonary vessels by a dislodged blood clot). Poultices or bandages with Manuka honey MGO100+ can counteract the inflammation, but honey injections would have a more immediate effect. Good results have been achieved with normal blossom honey, but Manuka honey is even more effective. Plenty of exercise and drinking enough water help prevent the risk of disease, while sitting for long periods and taking birth control pills increase it. See → Leg ulcers

Varicose veins | See → Venous inflammation

W

Warts | As warts are usually caused by viruses, they can be treated with Manuka products. Pure Manuka oil is particularly suitable. Dab the wart several times a day. Results should be seen in a few weeks.

Wounds | Apply Manuka honey MGO100+ directly to the clean wound and surrounding area or use an appropriately sized wound dressing soaked in Manuka honey. Change the dressing at least daily in the beginning. In the case of chronically infected wounds, especially if hospital bacteria are involved, the Manuka honey first creates a sterile wound environment before the healing process starts. This can take a little longer, but patience is usually rewarded. See also → Diabetic foot syndrome, → Pressure sores and → Leg ulcers

Y

Yeast infection | See → Candida albicans

MANUKA HONEY RECIPES

Even on its own, Manuka honey is a rich cocktail of some 200 active ingredients that complement and reinforce one other. But that synergy can also be achieved if you mix the honey with other natural ingredients. The following recipes show you how to use the honey in a pleasant and effective manner in combination with established natural remedies.

MIX'S BEE BALM – MY FAVOURITE ALL-PURPOSE OINTMENT

Ingredients
All ingredients should be organic wherever possible

80 ml	olive oil
20 ml	avocado oil
20 g	pure beeswax (I use fresh 'uncapping wax', the best quality beeswax available)
20 g	Manuka honey (MGO100+ or stronger) (approx. 1 heaped tsp.)
10 ml	alcohol-free propolis solution
10 drops	pure Manuka oil

Preparation

Heat the oil in a jar (I use brown 500 g honey jars and double the amount of everything) lowered into hot water (make sure the jar isn't cold when you immerse it, otherwise it will crack in the heat).

Grate the wax into small pieces and add to the oil so that it dissolves. Remove the jar from the hot water and stir in the honey, propolis solution and Manuka oil one after the other using a wooden spoon.

Continue to stir during the cooling process until the mixture coagulates. Once completely cooled, fill it into smaller containers. The ratio of wax to oil results in a consistency that won't become too hard or too soft even when temperatures fluctuate in summer and winter.

This ointment can be used as a lip balm and for skin inflammations, insect bites and sunburn. I even use it as a sunscreen. Maybe Manuka honey and the carbohydrate dihydroxyacetone (DHA) it contains play a role in this.

MANUKA OXYMEL

Ingredients

250 g   Manuka honey (e.g. MGO100+)
100 ml   naturally cloudy organic apple vinegar

Preparation

Oxymel, i.e. sour honey, is currently experiencing a renaissance. Oxymel simplex is a mixture of honey and vinegar that combines the beneficial properties of both natural substances and enhances them. Both are very good at extracting nutrients from herbs, berries and spices. Hildegard von Bingen was by no means the first to praise its effect 900 years ago. The oldest mention goes back to Pythagoras of Samos, who lived about 2500 years ago. Don't worry, no maths exam, just some ratio figures perhaps. Mix at a ratio of 5:2 honey to vinegar. For normal honey, I simply take 500 g honey and mix it with 200 ml vinegar. With Manuka honey, you can try it out with a smaller quantity, such as 250 g honey and 100 ml vinegar.

Stir this basic mixture thoroughly with a wooden or plastic spoon in a sealable jar and repeat this process for two to three days until there is no more honey at the bottom of the jar. You can enjoy this mixture pure or dissolve it like syrup in a glass of water and drink it. The option of using it to make tinctures is more interesting.

Cut approx. 30 g of 'cough' herbs such as coltsfoot, thyme, ribwort or sage, preferably fresh, into small pieces in roughly equal proportions and stir into the basic mixture. Garlic, onions and horseradish could also be added. The effect of these ingredients compensates for the unfamiliar taste. Leave to infuse for 14 days and stir daily. Then strain through a fine plastic sieve and pour into a dark bottle. A shot of this can safely be added to hot water before drinking.

There are an infinite number of possible combinations. Here are two of my favourites.

GINGER & TURMERIC OXYMEL

Ingredients

Oxymel

15 g	organic fresh ginger
15 g	organic fresh turmeric
	Half an organic lemon (sliced or juiced)

Optionally add

Half an organic vanilla bean pod, finely chopped

Half tsp. coarsely ground or crushed organic black pepper

Preparation

Wash the ginger and turmeric tubers, grate them (unpeeled) and mix with the other ingredients. Stir daily during the two-week extraction phase and then pour through a plastic sieve, pressing the solids with a spoon. (The pomace can be re-used: I usually dry it out a little and use it as a snack. It is deliciously sweet and sour with a refreshing sharpness and rich in fibre). This oxymel will keep for a long time even without refrigeration if it wasn't so delicious!

This blend supports the immune system, bile function and much more. A shot of this in a glass of water can be enjoyed with food, at work, exercise or whenever. I always carry a litre of this with me on my hikes.

POLLEN CINNAMON OXYMEL

Ingredients
Oxymel
25 g   pollen
15 g   sunflower lecithin
25 g   organic cinnamon

Preparation

Mix the ingredients together and leave to infuse for a few days. This can be done in a dark glass bottle,

as the mixture should be shaken before each use. The lecithin is a good emulsifier, but some sediment will always settle out at the top and bottom.

This energy drink contains the protein-rich, mood-lifting power of pollen and cinnamon, which does not only have an aromatic taste, but is also said to help balance insulin and to have an antimicrobial effect in the intestines and bladder. It also supports the cardiovascular system, possibly due to its coumarin content, which is significantly higher in the Chinese variety (cassia) than in Ceylon cinnamon. Coumarin (from which phenprocoumon is derived) is often prescribed to cardiovascular patients as a blood thinner.

I take a tablespoonful of the drink every now and then and let it slowly dissolve in my mouth. Otherwise just mix it with cold or occasionally hot water.

You can also mix 1 teaspoon of cinnamon powder with 1 tablespoon of Manuka honey and take it pure. The same applies to turmeric powder. Turmeric honey is highly praised as a natural antibiotic.

GOLDEN MILK WITH MANUKA HONEY

Turmeric is the key ingredient here too. Manuka honey mainly provides sweetness, but of course also contributes all its other good qualities. First, we make a turmeric paste.

Ingredients
For the paste:

1 cup	*organic turmeric powder*
3 cups	*water*
1 tsp.	*finely ground organic black pepper*

Turmeric is a relative of the ginger root. The addition of pepper makes the curcumin in turmeric easier to absorb. This is due to the piperine contained in the pepper. I also add three other ingredients from the same family:

1 Tbsp	*organic ginger*
1 tsp.	*organic galangal*
1 tsp.	*organic cardamom*

The first three ingredients are obligatory, the other three are optional.

Preparation

Mix everything in a saucepan and simmer for approx. 7 minutes over medium heat. The finished paste should be fairly dry and thick with little to no water. Place in a sealable jar and allow to cool. It can then be stored in the fridge for several weeks. This method using heat makes the turmeric more bio-available.

Ingredients
For each cup of Golden Milk:

200 ml	*organic full-fat milk or vegan milk substitute*
1 tsp.	*organic coconut oil*
1 tsp.	*turmeric paste*
½ tsp.	*Manuka honey*

Preparation

Heat the milk with the coconut oil, but do not boil. Add the turmeric paste and honey, mix well and drink hot.

MANUKA HONEY WITH ALOE VERA

Aloe vera is revered as the queen of medicinal plants. It has a reputation of being 'a whole pharmacy in one plant', because it comprises several hundred active ingredients like Manuka honey. A combination of the two is an incredible edible power-couple. Aloe vera tastes very bitter and even a large amount of honey can't hide this. Both internally and externally, this mixture can help treat inflammations and infections. Burns and even cancer have been referred to as possible candidates for treatment. The honey is not just there for its taste and preserving properties: it is believed to double the effect of the aloe vera.

Ingredients

150 g	fresh aloe vera, species Linné or arborescens
250 g	Manuka honey
2 Tbsp.	rum

Preparation

I always rely on my organic aloe plants, which I have had for years. They have grown quite big and hardly need any care. I cut off a suitable leaf from the bottom, wash it, remove the thorny edges and put it in a blender with the honey.

Blend everything finely, put it in a jar, add the rum and keep it sealed in the fridge. The mixture is very liquid and the aloe particles will settle on the surface, so shake before use. You may also want to shake after use. It is best to take a spoonful of this bitter-sweet medicine 15 minutes before each meal. This improves digestion and is even said to help fight cancer.

Even if you don't have an acute health or cosmetic problem to treat with Manuka honey, you can give yourself and your immune system a treat with this exquisite natural product. This also works if you combine it with a healthy breakfast.

LAST BUT NOT LEAST

Manuka honey – the real deal

Manuka truth and fake juice –
to what extent is this a problem?

Whenever there appears to be a discrepancy between the amount of Manuka honey sold worldwide and the amount actually produced in New Zealand, two figures are always mentioned: 10,000 tonnes are allegedly sold per year, although production of the honey is said to be no higher than 1,700 tonnes. But these figures, which have even been published on Wikipedia, are clearly false. The three biggest producers in New Zealand alone are responsible for about 3,000 to 4,000 tonnes of this delicacy, and the alleged counterfeiters naturally don't publish any figures.

Given the honey's price tag, there is no doubt that there have been and continue to be cases of forgery, from the addition of artificial methylglyoxal to counterfeit labels.

The amount of honey actually produced has obviously changed over the years because demand is so high, and the trade is so lucrative. On the other hand, the harvest of any natural product is subject to natural variation. Observers of the New Zealand honey trade believe that annual Manuka production is around 5,000 tonnes, although exact figures are hard to come by.

If you are going to spend a lot of money on Manuka products for the sake of your health, you obviously want to be sure that you are buying a genuine product, not one that has simply been repackaged. Manuka honey represents a significant income stream for New Zealand, and genuine producers as well as the New Zealand government, in the form of the Ministry for Primary Industries (MPI), have a vested interest in being able to prove the authenticity of their product.

Manuka security attracts government interest

The New Zealand government has recently created a set of regulations to protect Manuka honey as a valuable export commodity.

On the basis of specific markers, a distinction is made between pure Manuka honey (monofloral) and

Manuka honey mixed with other nectars (multifloral, i.e. weaker in effect). These are chemical components and genetic features by means of which the honeys can be clearly distinguished and identified as genuine. The fact that methylglyoxal is not one of the chemical markers may be due to the fact that this value is open to manipulation. To keep things simple, here is the table published by the New Zealand Ministry of Agriculture.

Four chemical compounds must be present:

Test for	Monofloral		Multifloral	
3-phenyllactic acid	Min.	400 mg/kg	Min.	20 mg/kg
2-methoxyaceto-phenone	Min.	5 mg/kg	Min.	1 mg/kg
2-methoxyben-zoic acid	Min.	1 mg/kg	Min.	1 mg/kg
4-hydroxyphe-nyllactic acid	Min.	1 mg/kg	Min.	1 mg/kg

In addition, a genetic test for the presence of Manuka pollen DNA is prescribed for both honeys.

A question of faith – UMF or MGO?

Qualities such as speed can be described comparatively – as fast as a cheetah or as slow as a turtle – but in general one uses a measurable unit of distance and time, i.e. kilometres per hour. James Watt called a unit of force horsepower (hp) and today the internationally recognised unit is the kilowatt (kW). Such standard units of measurement mean that power can be reliably measured.

There is a formula for the conversion of hp into kW. When measuring the strength of Manuka honey, a comparison of the UMF and MGO measurements can only ever be approximate. When MGO content is measured, absolute and reproducible values are obtained (i.e. x mg methylglyoxal per kg honey).

Prof Henle made this point when he gave a lecture to an audience of experts in New Zealand on the tenth anniversary of his discovery of MGO. "If you want to determine how drunk different drinkers are, you can compare how each of them walks in a line or how much their speech is impaired. But you could also simply measure their blood alcohol levels."

The term UMF describes efficacy against bacteria compared to the chemical antiseptic phenol, i.e. the "drunkenness level". Honeys with an MGO value simply state the amount of the active ingredient methylglyoxal in mg/kg, or the "alcohol content".

Strict regulations preventing honey fraud
Manipulation designed to accelerate conversion of dihydroxyacetone (DHA, see p. 16) to MGO, as well as the wrong storage conditions (too warm), can lead to a reduction in quality, or even withdrawal from sale if the honey has been denatured by heating and, as a result, valuable enzymes are destroyed, and undesirable by-products are produced. Experts refer to insufficient diastase and invertase values and increased HMF values (hydroxymethylfurfural).

Whether a honey is allowed to be marketed and consumed is strictly regulated by means of maximum and minimum values and laboratory controls. In the case of Manuka honeys that are not packaged and sealed in the country of production, the right measures need to be in place to ensure compliance, especially the avoidance of strong light and heat. Honeys packaged in Germany or Europe have few problems meeting the quality requirements, especially since they also have to comply with Europe's own strict honey regulations. Reputable suppliers will be able to provide the details of the relevant nutritional analysis, in some cases via a QR code on the jar.

CONCLUSION

Look out for the term methylglyoxal (MGO). Honeys bottled in New Zealand occasionally still have the UMF value on the label. The proof that you are buying an original product made and packaged in New Zealand is the silver fern mark. This is due to the government initiative under which producers have to meet strict criteria. The symbol, with the licence number also printed on the label, guarantees that you are buying an authentic New Zealand product. When it comes to honey quality, trust suppliers who are well established; experience shows that the authorities will eventually catch up with the fraudsters and put them out of business.

INDEX

A

Abscess	81
Acid	41, 42, 91
Acne	62, 81, 86
Allergies	37, 81
Aloe vera	116
Ammonia	41, 42
Antibacterial	17, 62
Antibiotic effect, selective	28, 87
Antibiotic resistance	21, 53
Antibiotics	20, 21, 30, 32, 33, 41, 42
Anti-inflammatory	34, 44, 62, 86
Antimicrobial	15, 16, 33, 42, 44, 55, 66, 67, 68, 70, 86, 113
Aphthae (mouth ulcers)	28, 94
Arthritis	81
Asthma	82, 83
Athlete's foot	70, 82, 95

B

Bacteria	20-24, 28, 32, 33, 37, 41, 42, 53-55, 60, 65, 66, 67, 122
Bees	10, 16, 47, 65, 67, 68, 70, 82
Bifidobacteria	67
Biofilm	32, 33, 55, 98, 99
Bladder	23, 46, 48, 113
Bladder infection	29, 67, 83, 85. 96, 101
Bronchitis	83, 85
Burns	59, 60, 84, 116

C

Calendula oil	63
Cancer	38, 84, 116, 117
Candida albicans	84, 103
Caries	85, 99, 100
Catalysis	48
Cells/Cell division	32, 54
Chemotherapy	21, 38, 94
Cinnamon	112
Colitis ulcerosa	44, 86, 88, 92, 100
Conjunctivitis	85
Contact	23, 30, 67
Cook, James	14, 70
COPD	37
Corona virus	38
coughing	37, 40
coumarin	113
Counterfeit honey	10, 118
Couperose	85
Crohn's disease	44, 86, 92

D

Demodex mite	86
Depression	87
Diabetics	46, 65
Diarrhoea	41, 86, 87
Digestive tract	41, 46, 69, 86
Dihydroxyacetone (DHA)	16, 42, 107, 122
Dihydroxyacetone phosphate (DHAP)	16
Diverticulitis	44, 88, 92
Duodenal ulcer	41, 88, 91

E

Eczema	89
Energy drink	113

Erysipelas 85
Eye inflammation 64, 85, 88, 92, 99

F
Fever 37
First-pass effect 46
Fleming, Alexander 20
Flu 89
Food Chemistry 16, 75
Foot syndrome, diabetic 59, 87, 93, 103
Fungi 55, 66, 67

G
Gastritis 41, 90, 91
Genetic test 121
Genital herpes 90
Gingivitis 90, 94, 96, 99
Golden milk 114
Granulation layer 55
Green tea 49, 83, 84, 96
Gums 29, 30, 90, 96, 101
Gut 23, 41, 44, 45, 61, 88

H
Haemorrhoids 90
Hay fever 90
Healing process 55, 64, 103
Heartburn 91, 95
Helicobacter pylori 24, 41, 42, 86, 88, 90, 91, 92, 99, 101
Henle, Thomas 16, 21, 42, 75, 77, 121
Herpes 64, 90, 92, 94, 98
Honey injections 65, 102
Hordeolum 92, 99

Hospital bacteria 92, 102
Hydroxymethyl-
furfural (HMF) 122
Hydroxyphenyllactic acid 120
Hyposensitisation 90, 96

I
Immune system 37, 38, 55, 61, 80, 81, 85, 111, 117
Infection 20, 30, 31, 32, 57, 65, 67, 80, 93, 94, 96, 101, 103
Inflammation 24, 25, 28, 30, 32, 44, 45, 70, 80
Inflammation of the
eyes 64
gums 30, 90, 96
intestinal wall 44
muscous
membran 38, 41
oesophagus 40
pancreas 95
skin 70
stomach lining 91
Inhalation 35
Itching 91

K
keloid formation 56
Keratitis 85, 93
Kidneys 46, 48
Klinik Havelhöhe 11
Kuhfuß, Reinhard 74, 77

L
Lactic acid 44
Lactic acid bacteria 67
Lactobacilli 67

Laryngitis 93
Larynx 40, 93
Leg ulcers 59, 93, 101, 103
Leptospermum
    scoparium 14, 70
Liver 46, 47, 48
Liver oil 20
Lungs 36, 39, 61
Lyme disease 93, 94, 100

M
Manuka bush/Manuka plant 10, 11, 16, 70
Manuka oil 33, 36, 62, 70, 82, 85, 95, 102, 106
Manuka Pioneers 74
Maori 10, 14
Medical product 59
Melaleuca alternifolia 70
Methoxyacetophenone 120
methoxybenzoic acid 120
Methylglyoxal (MGO) 16, 17, 22, 23, 25, 41, 42, 44, 57, 66, 75, 77, 85, 118, 120, 121, 123
Microbes 30
Microbiome 66
Molan, Peter 15
Monofloral 119, 120
Mood enhancer 87, 113
Mouth lining 94, 99, 101
MPI 119
Mucositis 38, 91, 94, 99

N
Nail fungus 70, 82, 95
Neurodermatitis 64, 86, 89, 95, 97

Neuseelandhaus 74, 75
New Zealand 10, 14, 17, 68, 77, 118, 123
Nose 30, 97

O
Oesophagitis 40, 91, 95
Oesophagus 39, 94
Ointment 63, 107
Opportunists 64
Osmotic 28, 54, 55, 94
Oxymel 108, 110, 112

P
Pain 34, 41, 55, 61, 75, 87, 90, 98
Pancreatitis 95
Pathogens 30, 37, 52, 59, 66, 68, 94
Pepsin 41, 42
Periodontitis 30, 96
Pharyngitis 96
Pharynx 37
Phenol 17, 122
Phlebitis 96, 101
Piperine 114
Pollen 47, 82, 87, 91, 95, 97, 112, 121
Pollen allergy 90, 96
Pork 89
Pressure sores 83, 93, 96, 103
Probiotic 55
Propolis 63, 64, 67, 82-101, 106
Prostatitis 49, 96
Psoriasis 62, 97

Q

Quality tests	74, 122

R

Rhinitis	97
Rhinosinusitis	32,097, 98
Rollkur ("Rolling cure")	24, 42, 91
Rosacea	85, 98
Royal jelly	87, 89, 97

S

Sage	93, 100, 109
Saliva	23, 28, 90
Scars	56
Secondary bacterial infections	86
Shingles	92, 98
Side-effects	9, 21, 38, 84, 87
Silver fern mark	123
Sinusitis	32, 97, 98
Sore throat	93, 94, 96, 99, 100
Staphylococcus infection	65
Stomach	23, 41, 70
Stomach lining	42, 43, 93
Stomach ulcer	91, 101
Stomatitis	28, 30, 94, 99
Storage	16, 122
Storage organ	46
Stress	90, 93, 100
Styes	92, 93
Sunflower lecithin	112
Sydney	21
Synergistic	33
Synergy	49, 105

T

Tampon	67, 83, 85, 91
Tea tree oil	70
Tendonitis	75
Tonsillitis	100
Toothpaste	85
Transamination	48
TU Dresden	16, 41, 75
Turmeric	110, 114

U

Ulcus cruris	93, 101
Ulcus ventriculi	99, 101
Unique Manuka Factor (UMF)	16, 17, 75, 121, 123
Urease	41, 42
Urethra	67

V

Vaginal yeast infection	67, 84
Varicose veins	90, 101, 102
Vascular inflammation	101
Venous inflammation	96, 100, 101, 102
Viruses	32, 37, 55, 64, 66, 89, 98, 102
Vital substances	55
Vocal cords	40

W

Water retention	54
Windpipe	39
Wound dressing	23, 55, 56, 57, 102
Wound environment	55, 102
Wound healing	59, 69, 102
Wound-healing honey	60
Wounds	20, 23, 53, 92, 102

You can get Manuka honey at local pharmacies, health stores or online.